生命的意義與日記中的答案
The Meaning of Life and the Answers in the Diary

（中英雙語版）
(Chinese-English Bilingual Edition)

決長
Jue Chang

美商EHGBooks微出版公司
www.EHGBooks.com

EHG Books 公司出版
Amazon.com 總經銷
2024 年版權美國登記
未經授權不許翻印全文或部分
及翻譯為其他語言或文字
2024 年 EHGBooks 第一版

Copyright © 2024 by Jue Chang
Manufactured in United States
Permission required for reproduction,
or translation in whole or part.
Contact: info@EHGBooks.com

ISBN-13：978-1-66580-002-0

目錄

目錄 1

序 5

生命的意義與日記中的答案。... 7

    壹、前言。... 7
    貳、「今天」是如同飢餓的「空白」。............................. 8
    參、日記中的答案。.. 10
        一、人類有吃飯的需求。.................................... 11
        二、人類有運動的需求。.................................... 12
        三、人類有娛樂的需求。.................................... 13
    肆、另一個證明的方法。.. 15
    伍、比較與應用。.. 15
        一、人為什麼應該思考？.................................... 15
        二、為什麼大學要有通識教育？.............................. 16
        三、文學是有意義的。...................................... 16
        四、愛國的理由。.. 17
        五、共通的中心思想。...................................... 17
        六、人工智能的崛起。...................................... 17
        七、父母的願望。.. 18
    陸、結論。.. 18

我們是誰？生命的意義與認同感。...................................... 19

    壹、前言。.. 19
    貳、相同點。.. 20
    參、另一個答案。.. 21

肆、什麼是善？..22
　　伍、筆者的答案。..25
　　陸、比較與應用。..26
　　　　一、忠誠與民主的爭論。..................................26
　　　　二、上帝說。..27
　　　　三、孔子。..27
　　　　四、愛台灣。..28
　　　　五、查核事實。..28
　　　　六、善的理由。..28
　　　　七、自殺的新聞。..29
　　柒、結語。..29

生命的意義與民主的圖騰....................................31

　　壹、前言。..31
　　貳、民主是價值嗎？..32
　　參、客觀的證明。..33
　　肆、龍的圖騰。...34
　　伍、廣播器的功用。..35
　　陸、新的圖騰。...35
　　柒、結論。..36

Preface...37

The Meaning of Life and the Answers in the Diary.................39

    Section 1 ：Introduction...39
    Section 2 ："Today" is a "blank" like hunger.......................40
    Section 3 ：Answers in the diary..43
        1. Human beings have the need to eat..............................44
        2. Human beings have a need for exercise......................46
        3. Human beings have entertainment needs....................47
    Section 4 ：Another way to prove.......................................49
    Section 5 ：Comparison and application............................50
        1. Why should people think?..50
        2. Why do universities need general education?............51
        3. Literature is meaningful...52
        4. Reasons for patriotism...52
        5. A Common Core Idea...53
        6. The rise of artificial intelligence..................................53
        7. Parents' wishes...54
    Section 6 ：Conclusion..54

Who are we? The meaning of life and identity.......................56

    Section 1 ：Preface..56
    Section 2 ：The common points of life..............................57
    Section 3 ：Another answer..59
    Section 4 ：What is goodness?...60
    Section 5 ：The author's answer..63
    Section 6 ：Comparison and application............................64
        1. The debate between loyalty and democracy................65
        2. God said..65

3. Confucius. 66
   4. Love Taiwan. 67
   5. Check the facts. 67
   6. Reasons for goodness. 68
   7. News of suicide. 68
   Section 7 : Conclusion. 69

The meaning of life and the symbol of democracy. 70

   Section 1 : Preface. 70
   Section 2 : Is democracy a value? 71
   Section 3 : Objective proof. 72
   Section 4 : The Loong's Symbol. 73
   Section 5 : Function of broadcaster. 75
   Section 6 : New Symbol. 76
   Section 7 : Conclusion. 77

序

生命的意義是人類歷史上最難的題目,
學校說這問題不會有標準答案。
真是奇怪啊!
生命不確定有沒有意義,
但是上學有意義?
老師站到講台上,
然後說:「我說的話沒有意義。」
真是奇怪的事。

筆者發現了一件簡單而重要的事,
「今天要做什麼呢?」
這就代表著人們必須填飽今天,
人們必須為「今天」負責,
筆者發現了生命有意義。

「人們必須填滿今天。」
但這答案太抽象了,
具體而言要填入什麼呢?
所以本篇文章有很多例子。
「人們必須為今天負責。」
所以老師應該告訴學生們:
「你應該為你的人生負責。」
學校應該告訴學生善的觀念。

而善的觀念會造成巨大的影響。

具體例子、善的觀念、文字的影響。
本書的內容就是這三個題目：
「生命的意義與日記中的答案。」
「我們是誰？生命的意義與認同感。」
「生命的意義與民主的圖騰。」

筆者想要告訴大家：
以前生命不確定有沒有意義，
現在生命真的有意義。

決長

2023、10、01

生命的意義與日記中的答案。

壹、前言。

　　人活著要做什麼呢？生命的意義是什麼呢？這是人類歷史中最難的題目，曾經有哲學家們認真挑戰這題目，但失敗後發瘋了，但失敗後自殺了，當有青少年認真思考生命的意義時，父母會感到擔心，希望子女不要想太多，淺淺地想就好，千萬不要深入地想。

　　而在日常生活中，筆者發現了：「人活著要做什麼？這是一個容易、輕鬆的題目。」

　　筆者不是新生的嬰兒，「今天要做什麼呢？週末要做什麼呢？連續假期要做什麼呢？」筆者已經回答很多次這問題了，下一個「今天」不是未知的，日記中已經有「今天」的答案了。

　　肚子餓了，和同事隨便找了間餐廳吃午餐，「今天要做什麼呢？」，這是容易的題目，和選擇午餐一樣容易，本篇文章將說明：
　　一、「今天」是如同飢餓的「空白」。
　　二、日記中的答案。
　　三、另一個證明方法。
　　四、比較與應用。

　　日記中，我已經填滿了「今天」，
　　本篇文章將說明：「具體而言，今天要做什麼呢？」
　　本篇文章將說明成對的飢餓與美好。

貳、「今天」是如同飢餓的「空白」。

為什麼人類要思考生命的意義這題目呢？
在過去，人類誤解了這題目，
生命的意義是一個崇高的題目，
所以平庸的人不用思考這題目。
生命的意義是接近天堂的方向，
所以不相信神的人不用思考這題目。
「意義」是人類主觀強加的想法，
因為人類胡思亂想、內心不安，想著、想著，因為不安，所以為生命強加了「意義」，但「沒意義」又如何？為什麼一定要「有意義」呢？
這是人類對這題目的誤解。

而筆者發現：「生命有意義，人類必須填飽今天。」
今天是等待填入的空白，
而空白中藏著飢餓，
所以每個人都要回答「今天」，人類會餓，人類必須填飽今天。
以下是「人類必須填飽今天」的實驗方法：

實驗一：
一、準備相同的兩個房間，房間 A 和房間 B。
二、準備兩位志願者，一位進入房間 A，一位進入房間 B。將房門鎖上。
三、準備攝影機拍攝志願者。
四、每隔四個小時送一些食物進入房間 A，房間 B 沒有食物。
五、記錄志願者是否有憤怒、痛苦的反應。

這是簡單的實驗，這個實驗可以觀測到飢餓，這是「今天」的特性，今天要做什麼呢？今天有我必須要做的事，今天我要吃飯。

實驗二：
一、準備相同的兩個籠子，籠子 A 和籠子 B。
二、準備兩隻狗（或兩位人類的志願者），一隻進入籠子 A，一隻進入籠子 B，將籠子鎖上。
三、為兩個籠子（A 和 B)準備充足的食物和水。
四、準備攝影機拍攝狗。
五、每天將籠子 A 的狗帶出籠子外，散步一個小時，然後再關回籠子 A。而籠子 B 的狗不能散步。
六、記錄狗的健康狀況（食慾、活動力、睡眠、心跳、血氧……）。

這是簡單的實驗，這個實驗可以證明：「狗（人類）有運動的需求。」
這是「今天」的特性，今天要做什麼呢？
今天有我必須要做的事，今天我要運動。

實驗三：
一、準備兩個空無一物的房間，房間 A 和房間 B。
二、準備兩位志願者，一位進入房間 A，一位進入房間 B，鎖上房門。
三、在兩個房間內放入足夠的食物和水，再放入各一台跑步機。
四、在房間 A 放入一台可以上網的手機，房間 A 內的志願者可以打電話給朋友，而房間 B 沒有手機。
五、讓志願者在房間內生活一個月。

六、滿一個月時,為志願者做健康檢查(食慾、活動力、睡眠、心跳、血氧、記憶力……)。

這是簡單的實驗,這個實驗可以證明:「人類需要娛樂,人類有情感上的需求。」

這是「今天」的特性,今天要做什麼呢?

今天有我必須要做的事,今天我要尋找娛樂,今天我要尋找愛與歡笑。

藉由這三個實驗,可以證明:「今天」有特性,今天我要吃飯,今天我要運動,今天我要尋找娛樂,「今天」等著人類填入色彩,和飢餓一樣無法拒絕,人類必須為「今天」填入色彩,只要人類還存活於地球上,人類必須為「今天」填入色彩。

參、日記中的答案。

在舊觀念中,未來是未知的,人生是未知的,你認為確定的事也許明天就變了。

而筆者發現了:「人類必須為今天填入色彩。」這件事在未來還會是對的,

筆者在自己的日記中、在自己的書中寫著:「人生有答案,這是已知的,人類必須為今天填入色彩。」

人類必須為今天填入色彩,那麼具體而言要填入什麼呢?答案是:「都可以。」,但「都可以」不是一個具體的答案,所以在這個小節,筆者將拿出自己的日記和人類的歷史中做過的事當例子,這些事都是「人類必須為今天填入色彩」的答案。

一、人類有吃飯的需求。

今天要吃什麼呢？答案是「都可以」，具體而言我吃過什麼呢？翻開日記，我吃過了：炒飯、炒麵、麵包、漢堡、三明治、包子、饅頭、水餃、油條、烤地瓜、炸芋頭、泡芙、披薩、麻婆豆腐、巧克力、冰淇淋、銅鑼燒、壽司、珍珠奶茶、豆漿、果凍、布丁、沙拉、蜂蜜蛋糕、鏡面蛋糕、榴槤、海苔飯捲、粽子、湯圓、咖哩、甜甜圈、糖葫蘆、洋芋片、皮蛋、粥、美乃滋翠筍、羊羹、味增湯、泡麵、鳳梨酥、沙其馬、爆米花、火鍋、拉麵、通心麵、麥片、刨冰、豆花、鬆餅、熱狗、香腸、玉米濃湯、芝麻糊、藥膳湯、松露鮮菇湯……

翻開日記，我吃過了什麼呢？

我喜歡吃軟的高麗菜，我的媽媽常常為我做特別的高麗菜料理，特別軟、特別細，是在所有餐廳都吃不到的特殊料理。

曾經，和我的朋友在一個偏僻的山上，隨便找了一間路邊的咖啡廳，沒想到遇到了超級好喝的咖啡，把我和朋友都嚇到了。

曾經，我和我的社團夥伴去露營，用卡式爐煮著麵，有夥伴抱怨麵不夠，就往鍋子中加了麵，於是鍋子中就有太熟的舊的麵和不熟的新的麵，那是充滿歡笑的一餐。

有一間我常去的咖啡廳，因為太常去了，所以我把他們菜單上的所有口味都試了一遍。

記得小時候，半夜在客廳吃泡麵，騙我爺爺說是太餓睡不著，其實是有想看的節目……

日記中都是生命的意義的答案。

在日記中，筆者記得，佛陀說：天堂重要，吃飯不重要。筆者記得，學者們爭論著利與義，追逐利益的是小人，追逐自由與價值的是君子，商人說：民主不能當飯吃。民主先烈說：民主像空氣，雖然不能當飯吃但是很重要。

而筆者發現了：「吃飯真的很重要。」

因為吃飯真的很重要，所以我要感謝農夫、感謝廚師、感謝司機、感謝麵包店的收銀員......

因為吃飯真的很重要，所以我們要關心稅金、關心國家，人民要叫國家照顧人民。

日記中有生命的意義的答案，吃飯真的很重要，我們要關心國家，我們要一起吃飯。

在歷史中，為了吃飯，人類發展了貿易，人類學會了合作。為了吃飯，人類發明了罐頭、冰箱、微波爐，農夫努力種出更好吃的水果，廚師想著新的菜單，筆者生活在便利的文明之中。

如何才能回答吃飯這個問題？豐富的菜單、進步的科技、互相關心的社會、便利的文明，文明就在我的眼前。具體而言，今天要填入什麼呢？歷史中有答案，眼前的文明就是具體的答案了。

二、人類有運動的需求。

今天要做什麼呢？答案是「都可以」，具體而言我做了什麼運動呢？

翻開日記，我做過了：跑步、籃球、棒球、足球、排球、桌球、網球、羽球、跳高、跳繩、跳遠、鉛球、溜溜球、拔河、太極拳、和同學用掃把對打、啦啦隊、爬樹、盪鞦韆、體操、游泳、抓迷藏、跳舞、騎腳踏車、溜冰、伏地挺身、甩手、躲避球、玩溜滑梯、玩蹺蹺板、按摩、划船......

翻開日記，筆者最常做的運動是散步和跑步。好無聊啊！筆者在國中的時候曾經這麼覺得，那時候還是填鴨教育，學校不鼓勵思考，學校鼓勵背誦，因為太無聊了，所以筆者去跑操場，真是適合啊，無聊的時候去做同學們認為無聊的事，筆者可以跑一萬公尺，時間是五十分鐘，調整呼吸、重複的動作、忘掉考試，筆者找到了快樂，這是一個偉大的發現，「如何抖去心中的煩悶？如何感到快樂？」這是許多學者在挑戰的題目，而筆者的日記中有答案。

翻開日記，筆者記得國中時的疑惑，介於小孩和大人之間，對未來的疑惑。筆者記得有一些同學也有相似的困擾，一樣對未來感到疑惑，充沛的體力卻不知道要將體力花在什麼地方，打架吧！飆車吧！尋求刺激吧！而老師是無力的，沒有人可以回答人生，沒有人可以回答未來。

這個難題有著簡單的答案，未來是確定的，筆者發現了：「人類需要運動。」這在未來還會是對的，這就是人生的答案。

你可以試著跑步，你可以試著打籃球，你可以試著去街上抓 AR 遊戲中的怪獸，答案是「都可以」，去試試看吧！

在圖書館的報紙中，記載著光輝的時刻，筆者的故鄉熱愛棒球，當國際賽時，我們有共通的感動。人生的答案是什麼？新聞中介紹著將人生獻給棒球的偉大選手。未來的答案是什麼？在未來，如果筆者的故鄉沒有滅亡，故鄉的人們還會繼續打棒球。人類已經不是原始人了，人類發明了棒球，具體而言，今天要填入什麼呢？棒球是具體的，棒球就是具體的答案了。

三、人類有娛樂的需求。

今天要做什麼呢？答案是「都可以」，我的心會餓，具體而言我為我的心靈填入了什麼呢？

　　翻開日記，我做過了：閱讀、寫作、攝影、塗鴉、看漫畫、看動畫、打電玩、下圍棋、看報紙、看電視、聽音樂、賞花、賞月、看煙火、捏陶土、折紙飛機、猜謎、變魔術、惡作劇、看相聲、看梗圖、玩骨牌、躲貓貓、撲克牌、吹泡泡、對著電風扇講話、科學小實驗、收集郵票、擼貓、逛街、欣賞別人的打扮、拜訪朋友、上網、左手拿著機器人右手拿著恐龍，讓機器人和恐龍戰鬥……

　　翻開手機的紀錄，在通訊軟體中，筆者的母親常常和我說早安，而我常常傳一些有趣的新聞給她，比如，小狗迷路了進警局求救，比如，動物園的熊站著走路被懷疑是工讀生裝扮的熊，比如，有笨蛋打電話去氣象局抱怨天氣太差……筆者的母親已經退休了，我教她如何使用手機，如何播放音樂，如何搜尋影片，有些書不用去圖書館，用手機就可以看了……要用什麼填滿心靈呢？這就是答案，通訊軟體中的早安就是答案了。

　　今天要做什麼呢？答案在圖書館裡，走進圖書館，櫃台邊有工作人員照顧的小花，美是今天的答案。報紙區有今天的新報紙，退休的老伯伯們排著隊，看看新聞，這是今天的答案。圖書館有新書區，館員向讀者推薦一些新書，圖書館有舊的經典，金斧頭銀斧頭的故事、三隻小豬的故事將會一直流傳。圖書館有學生在寫報告，如果題目是自由發揮，學生們會寫下什麼呢？

　　具體而言，今天要填入什麼呢？
　　去年的暑假和朋友去游泳然後去吃冰然後去逛夜市，今年暑假也要做一樣的事嗎？十年後的學生們也會做一樣的事嗎？
　　人的心會餓，古人們為心靈填入了什麼呢？古人們留下了經典，貝多芬、莫札特、莎士比亞……這就是具體的答案了，答案是音樂與文學,文學就是生命的意義的答案了。

肆、另一個證明的方法。

　　生命有沒有意義?這是人類歷史中最難的問題,在過去,沒有人可以證明有或沒有,而筆者證明了生命有意義,筆者提出了實驗的方法,可以證明大自然有法則,人類活著有必須要做的事,人類要吃飯、運動、填入娛樂、情感,筆者的實驗方法是可以用攝影機觀測的,但還是會有讀者感到懷疑,筆者舉了具體的例子,但還是會有讀者感到懷疑,人們總是對生命感到畏懼,答案已經在眼前了,還是會有讀者懷疑著:生命真的有意義嗎?決長解答了這問題了嗎?

　　除了事實,還有更好的說服別人的方法嗎?筆者已經拿出了事實,但人們的心中還是感到懷疑,所以,在這一個小節,筆者將提出另一個方法來證明生命有意義,方法如下:
　　只要我能否定:「生命沒意義」和「生命不確定有沒有意義」這兩句話,我就可以證明生命有意義了。

伍、比較與應用。

　　「生命的意義」這題目和日常生活相關,在日常生活中有許多應用,但「生命沒意義」這句話無法產生任何的應用,筆者發現了生命有意義,筆者的發現會帶來什麼改變呢?這個小節是比較與應用。

一、人為什麼應該思考?

　　在封建時代,國王教育人民服從,而在現在,學校鼓勵學生思考，為什麼服從是錯的而思考是對的？學校的老師們總是說：「生命沒有標準答案，老師們不是聖人，老師們沒有生命的答案，你們應該思考，你們應該找出自己的答案。」而這是錯誤的，「老師們沒有答案」這句話是沒有意義的，「老師們沒有答案」這句話只會推導出：思考不一定是對的。老師是笨蛋跟學生應該思考這兩件事完全沒有關係，只有「生命有意義，你應該充實心靈」這樣才能推導出「人應該思考」的這個結論。

二、為什麼大學要有通識教育？

為什麼大學要有通識課呢？通識課有意義嗎？當通識老師們提到生命的意義時，老師們總是說：「生命的意義是一個難題，有些人認為生命有意義，有些人認為生命沒有意義，而通識課程的目的就是帶領學生們聽聽雙方的意見。」真是奇怪呢！生命不確定有沒有意義，但是通識課有意義？「生命不確定有沒有意義」這句話是沒有意義的，「生命不確定有沒有意義」只會推導出：「尊重是沒有意義的。」應該是：「生命有意義，人要豐富心靈，人要豐富欣賞美的角度。」生命確定有意義，通識課才確定有意義，請通識老師們不要特地站到講台上，然後說通識課不確定有沒有意義。

三、文學是有意義的。

筆者發現了，文學是有意義的，這是一個簡單的發現，而文學家們有發現這件事嗎？很矛盾的，有些文學家說生命有意義，而有些文學家感嘆人生，感嘆著：努力了一輩子卻什麼都沒有留下，有些文學家說人生是虛無。真是奇怪呢！特地寫了文章，然後在文章中說人生沒意義，「這篇文章沒意義」，如果文學沒有意義，那麼學生們為什麼要接觸文學呢？

四、愛國的理由。

在獨裁國家中,國王會要求人民忠誠,而在民主國家中,你可以愛國,也可以不愛國,人生沒有標準答案,如果有一個人說他有標準答案,他說他代表著道德,他把一個道德標準強加在別人身上,那麼這個人是危險的,只有獨裁者和神棍才會說道德有標準答案。這是舊的觀念,這是矛盾的,民主國家的人民不用愛國,真是奇怪。筆者發現了人有吃飯的需求,我們要一起吃飯,我們要感謝農夫,我們要關心稅金,我們要關心國家,筆者找到了共通的答案。

五、共通的中心思想。

在民主國家中,每個人都可以提出自己的主張,是嗎?那麼,總統候選人可不可以把獨裁當成政見呢?如果主張獨裁的候選人當選了呢?這是可笑的事,當然,主張獨裁的人當選後國家就會走向獨裁,民主就會被消滅了,民主不能自我否定。如果我們沒有共通的中心思想,一半的人支持民主,一半的人支持獨裁,我們的國家將陷入紛亂。

而同樣的理由,民主不能自我否定,生命也不能自我否定,不能有一半的人認為生命沒有意義。

六、人工智能的崛起。

在科幻小說中常常有這樣的情節:「人工智能崛起,人類不用再工作了,看似幸福,但人類開始墮落、腐敗,然後進步的文明就自我滅亡了。」科幻小說中的這個題目可能快要成真了,面對人工智能的崛起,老師應該告訴學生們:「生命有意義,人必須鍛鍊自己,人必須充實心靈。」「生命有意義,我們要一起吃飯,我們要叫國家照顧跌倒的人，人們必須一直付出關心。」

七、父母的願望。

當迎接新生命時，父母會想像子女的未來，父母們會許下願望，而有一個常見的願望是：「我不會要求我的子女有什麼偉大的成就，只要他能平安長大，愛惜自己，然後要做什麼都可以。」願望是沒有根據的，而筆者證明了這件事，答案就是「都可以」，但是你必須要運動，你必須要珍惜自己。

陸、結論。

今天要做什麼呢？人活著要做什麼呢？筆者找到答案了，筆者發現了今天是如同飢餓的「空白」，這是可以用攝影機拍下的，人類有需求，人類需要吃飯、運動、填入娛樂與情感，人類必須要為今天填入色彩，而具體而言該填入什麼呢？筆者用日記中的答案來舉例了，筆者已經證明生命有意義了。

「生命沒意義」和「生命不確定有沒有意義」這兩句話不會有任何的應用，如果生命的意義和通識教育無關，那就請通識老師們不要提到生命的意義，如果生命的意義和通識教育有關，那就代表生命有意義，請通識老師們不要站到講台上，然後說我不知道，然後說：生命不確定有沒有意義，通識課不確定有沒有意義。請停止愚蠢的自我否定。

以前沒有人可以證明生命真的有意義，現在生命真的有意義，是誰解答了這問題呢？請大聲說出來：「生命真的有意義，決長解答了這難題。」

我們是誰？生命的意義與認同感。

壹、前言。

筆者的故鄉是台灣，台灣以前是威權的，台灣現在正走向民主，台灣有政治人物說：「民主是我們的 DNA。」

這是錯誤的，民主不是生而知之的事，

在過去，台灣人深愛著獨裁者，把獨裁者當成父母、救世主一般地愛著，

獨裁者曾經是老師們口中的英雄，父母告訴子女長大後要和那位英雄一樣偉大，

我們是誰？我們是獨裁者的子女、信徒。

哲學家們常說：生命的意義沒有共通的答案，每個人的答案不一樣。

這是錯誤的，生命的意義有共通的答案，生命的意義就是忠君愛國，犧牲小我，成就大我，有許多人願意為國王獻出生命。

聽神的話也是生命的意義的共通答案，以神之名，信徒們組成了大家庭，信徒們願意為了神獻出生命，獨裁者與神都曾經組成了大家庭。

在獨裁者的大家庭中，有人喊了自由，但自由是互不干涉嗎？

我們可以組成新的大家庭嗎？

「我們是誰？」這個問題有答案嗎？

本篇文章將說明：

一、生命的共通點。

二、我們要填入什麼？

三、什麼是善？

四、比較與應用。

「我們是誰？」就是如何為下一代建立完整的人格，本篇文章將說明「善的理由」、「團結的理由」。

貳、相同點。

「我們是誰？」哲學家說這是一個難題，

「我們應該成為怎樣的人？」

老師們說：每個人都是不同的，人生沒有標準答案。

這是一個矛盾，人生沒有標準答案，但是我們應該團結對抗獨裁。

為了解決這個矛盾，筆者發現了人類有共同點，以下是筆者的實驗方法：

一、只要準備實驗組和對照組，對照組是沒有食物的房間，實驗組每隔四個小時就送入一些食物，然後觀察房間內的志願者，這個實驗可以證明人類有共同點，每個人都會餓。

二、準備實驗組和對照組，對照組是空的房間，實驗組的房間有電視、漫畫和手機，然後觀察房間內的志願者，這個實驗可以證明，人類有共同點，人的心會餓，人類有情感的需求。

三、準備實驗組和對照組，

對照組是在地球生活的人類，
實驗組是在太空漂流的人類，
這個實驗可以證明，
人類需要土地，人類有共同點，
我們是地球人。

我們是誰？答案就在眼前，
我們可以觀察人類，
觀察後可以發現人類的特點，
人類會餓，
人類需要愛與歡笑，
人類需要土地、故鄉，
我們是誰？我們是地球人。

參、另一個答案。

我們是誰？
我們都曾經是嬰兒，
只會哭著要喝奶，
需要父母的呵護，
需要父母唱搖籃曲、說故事。
我們曾經像一張白紙，
不會說話，不會寫自己的名字，
白紙上沒有「我是誰？」的答案，
在接受了父母、老師的教育後，
在成長探索後，白紙不再是空白，

「我是誰?」「我們是誰?」
有另一個答案。

空白之中要填入什麼?
媽媽為我唱了民謠,在我的故鄉有幾首傳唱了很久的民謠,媽媽為我煮飯,有幾道常見的料理,在我的故鄉每個人都吃過相同的料理,三隻小豬的故事,龜兔賽跑的故事,媽媽跟我說了故事。
空白之中要填入什麼?
在學會說話後,
小孩子也學會了吵架與發脾氣,
於是媽媽必須要教小孩善與惡的觀念,
空白中要填入教育,
空白中要填入「什麼是善?」和「我們應該成為怎樣的人?」的答案。

肆、什麼是善?

什麼是善?什麼偉大?
我們應該成為怎樣的人?
媽媽給子女買了世界偉人傳記,
貝多芬、林肯、萊特兄弟、愛迪生、甘地、南丁格爾……
媽媽說這些是偉大的人,媽媽希望子女成為小小愛迪生。

什麼是善?
宗教是善,
耶穌、佛陀、阿拉和許多的神都是善,

以神之名，信徒們一起祈禱，吃飯前祈禱，睡覺前祈禱，為彼此祈禱，信徒們一起慶祝聖人的生日，信徒們一起唱聖歌，當失戀時，其他信徒們送上溫暖，當要填大學志願時，其他信徒會一起討論，當煩惱懊悔時，會有年長的信徒靜靜聆聽，當住院時，其他信徒會來探望，宗教團結著人們，神是善，人們是神的子女。

　　什麼是善？
　　愛國是善，自私是惡，
　　忠誠是善，質疑是惡。
　　不忠的將軍將帶來戰亂，
　　唯有忠誠是和平的答案。
　　不要自私，一切都屬於國王，
　　國王說：「我的子民啊！我的家園啊！你們是屬於我的，我愛你們。」
　　媽媽的故事書中有騎士的故事，
　　英勇的騎士，守護著國王與人民，
　　我們懷念著祖先，
　　祖父的祖父為了國家而犧牲了，
　　因為他們的犧牲才有現在的家園，
　　自私是懦弱而可恥的，
　　一個人的生命是渺小而無意義的，
　　只有為了國家而活，生命才有意義，
　　捨棄自我，化為群體，
　　我們是一體的，我們是國王的劍。

　　什麼是善？

國王是善，宗教是善？真的嗎？
　　人不能自私嗎？
　　再深入想想，
　　善有標準答案嗎？
　　善與惡常常因為立場而改變，
　　常常因為時間而改變，
　　未來是未知的，
　　人類沒有找到「真正的正義」。

　　白人至上是對的？
　　黑白平等是對的？
　　金恩博士說：「I have a dream.」
　　但夢想是無法證明的，
　　金恩博士沒有說他一定是對的。
　　生命有意義？生命沒意義？
　　當有高材生因為找不到生命的意義而自殺時，校長說：「老師們不是聖人，老師沒有人生的答案。」

　　你應該關心故鄉，
　　但人不能自私嗎？
　　民主是珍貴的，
　　但多數就是對的嗎？
　　你應該思考，
　　但人不能平庸嗎？
　　普世價值是一個謊言，
　　父母不該決定子女的人生，

你是你，我是我，

善沒有標準答案，

「我們是誰？」沒有答案。

伍、筆者的答案。

人類沒有找到真正的正義，

未來是未知的，人類沒有找到一定是對的事，

而筆者發現了：「未來是已知的。」

只要準備實驗組和對照組，

對照組維護環境，實驗組不維護環境，

這樣就可以證明人類應該維護地球，

這件事在一萬年後還會是對的。

只要準備實驗組和對照組，

可以證明人會餓，

人們要一起吃飯、一起維護故鄉。

只要準備實驗組和對照組，

可以證明人的心會餓，

人要思考，人要填入愛與歡笑。

筆者找到了真正的正義，

人要思考、人要關心故鄉、人要維護地球，這件事在一萬年以後還會是對的。

「我們是誰？」

小孩像白紙一般等待父母的教育，

父母要告訴小孩什麼可以做，什麼不可以做，父母要告訴小孩

善的觀念，

但人類有找到一定是對的事嗎？

人類可以找到一定是對的事然後告訴子女嗎？

有的，決長找到了，

只要準備實驗組和對照組可以證明：

人要思考、人要關心故鄉、人要維護地球。

當要填入健全的人格、善的觀念時，

我們要告訴下一代：

「科學證明了：人要思考、人要關心故鄉。」

代代相傳，我們流傳的是科學，

我們是科學人。

陸、比較與應用。

我們是誰？筆者發現了人類有共同點，

我們是地球人。

我們應該成為怎樣的人？我們要怎麼教育下一代？筆者發現了在未來還會是對的事，我們要告訴下一代：「只要準備實驗組和對照組，可以證明人應該思考、人應該關心故鄉。」

我們是科學人。

筆者的發現是簡單而重要的發現，

這個小節是比較與應用。

一、忠誠與民主的爭論。

在從威權走向民主的過程中，常常有這樣的場景，爺爺說國王對國家有重大的恩惠，而青少年喊著民主與自由，民主只是政治制度嗎？忠誠是信仰，推動民主就是要改變舊信仰，但矛盾地，民主是信仰自由，爺爺信仰著忠誠，青少年信仰著自由，自由應該包容忠誠。而民主先烈沒有說民主一定是對的，民主先烈說：人生沒有標準答案，我們要自由。

二、上帝說。

因為上帝與國王的旨意，所以你們要守法。因為國王是天選之人，所以你們要忠誠。

而當人們要追求自由的時候，民主先烈也說了類似的話：因為上帝說人權是對的、自由是對的、民主是對的，所以我們要民主。於是矛盾地，上帝是唯一的義，人民有信仰的自由。於是矛盾地，自由是人類的本能，在兩千年前人類就愛好自由，聖經寫著民主，是嗎？

三、孔子。

在中華文化中，孔子是最偉大的老師，是所有老師的老師，人們曾經和野獸一樣互相爭奪，在無秩序中，孔子說：「君王要有君王的樣子，臣子要有臣子的樣子，父親要有父親的樣子，子女要有子女的樣子。」孔子提倡「忠」、「孝」，我們應該聽國王與父母的話，孔子帶來了秩序，大部分的華人都是孔子的門生。

而在未來，我們要教育下一代「忠誠」還是「民主」？而孔子的書中沒有「民主」，我們還是孔子的門生嗎？

四、愛台灣。

筆者的故鄉是台灣,台灣曾經爭論著:「台灣人可以不愛台灣嗎?」

民主是自由,你可以關心故鄉,你也可以自私不愛台灣,人生沒有標準答案,但如果有人不愛台灣,他會被責罵:「你好大的膽子,你居然敢不愛台灣。」有一個矛盾,「人生沒有標準答案」跟「台灣人有共同的人生」是衝突的,而筆者找到了共通的答案,筆者找到了團結的理由。

五、查核事實。

金恩博士說:「I have a dream 」,

當人們在討論公共事務時,在舊觀念中,

沒有人是「中立、理性、客觀」,不要說謊了,你是主觀,我也是主觀,每個人都有他的立場,所以金恩博士分享他的夢想,如果很多人認同了他的夢想,他的夢想就可以形成政策。

而在新的觀念中,當眾人的意見出現歧異時,我們要檢查,意見是否符合事實,「事實」是整合眾人意見的依據。

六、善的理由。

我們應該成為怎樣的人?

父母告訴子女「善的理由」,

因為聖誕老人會送禮物,所以你要當個乖小孩,因為半夜會有虎姑婆,虎姑婆會吃不乖的小孩,所以你要當個乖小孩,耶穌和佛陀說了天堂與地獄,所以你要當個乖小孩,我們是誰?我們是聖誕老人喜歡的乖小孩,善的理由是童話。

而誰找到了真正的正義呢？
誰找到了善的理由呢？
筆者找到了，
筆者證明了：「人應該關心故鄉。」

七、自殺的新聞。

台灣大學重複著這樣的悲劇：
因為找不到生命的意義，所以有學生自殺了。
那麼老師們會怎麼教生命的意義呢？
生命的意義是千古難題，
沒有人能證明生命有沒有意義。
或是
生命真的有意義，
決長解答了這難題。

真是殘忍，許多老師不願意告訴學生「生命真的有意義」，
許多老師是耶穌、佛陀、孔子的門生，
所以他們不願意說出這個新觀念。

柒、結語。

我們是誰？
在過去，人們跪拜著，
人們是國王與上帝的子女，
而未來，人們還要繼續跪拜嗎？

你有你的信仰，我有我的信仰，
信仰是自由的，是嗎？
那學校要怎麼教育下一代呢？
善是忠誠、善是聽國王的話、善是回天堂，我們要怎麼教呢？

我們是誰？
人應該思考、應該關心故鄉，是嗎？
是的，我們是地球人，我們應該關心地球。
人應該思考、應該關心故鄉，真的嗎？
是的，只要準備實驗組和對照組，
可以證明此事為真，我們依循「Truth」，
我們是科學人。

生命的意義與民主的圖騰

壹、前言。

筆者的故鄉最近在進行選舉（2023、台灣），「捍衛普世價值，捍衛民主價值」，候選人這麼說，候選人之間比賽著，好像誰把「普世價值」喊得比較大聲，誰就代表著正義。

而普世價值到底是什麼？為什麼你們要為了主觀的價值而爭吵？在過去，曾經有烈士為了「民主價值」而犧牲，真是矛盾，民主是很珍貴的，民主是虛幻的價值。當公眾人物在台上說民主是主觀的價值時，台灣的學者並沒有出聲指正，學者們並不清楚民主是主觀或客觀。

民主只是一個抽象的詞，
只是一個被供奉的圖騰，
是嗎？
那麼供奉民主和供奉獨裁會有什麼不同呢？
民主可以讓人民吃飽嗎？
本篇文章將說明：「民主可以讓人民吃飽。」
本篇文章將設計民主的對照組和獨裁的實驗組，來證明民主。

本篇文章將說明：
一、以前民主是價值。
二、客觀的證明。
三、威權的圖騰。
四、新的圖騰。

本篇文章將說明圖騰就是「我們應該怎麼活？」的答案，

本篇文章將說明圖騰對生活造成的影響。

貳、民主是價值嗎？

民主是主觀的價值嗎？

民主確定是對的嗎？

人們說民主是普世價值，真是奇怪，主觀的價值不會有對與錯，真是奇怪，普世價值不是忠誠嗎？

在這個小節，筆者將說明：

「為什麼以前人們認為民主是價值？」

基於國王與上帝的旨意，人民應該守法，

在過去，國王就是善，國王也是財富的分配者，人民要向國王下跪才有飯吃，在跪著吃飯的時候，人民受到了欺凌，於是有人站出來反抗，他們喊著自由，他們不要飯也不要命，自由是價值，利與義是衝突的，追求利益的是小人，追求價值的是君子。

於是出現了一個矛盾，

有人說：「民主不能當飯吃。」

有人說：「民主是高貴的價值。」

「民主是高貴的價值不能當飯吃。」

人們認為民主是價值。

為什麼民主是價值？

因為忠誠是錯的，

人生沒有標準答案，
每個人都可以表達自己的看法，
而民主是主觀的看法、價值，
你可以支持獨裁，你也可以支持民主，
民主只是一個選擇。
未來是未知的，沒有人一定是對的，
多數決一定比聽國王的話好嗎？
不一定，
但是當面對未知的未來時，
先烈們相信民主，
民主是主觀的相信、選擇、看法、價值。

參、客觀的證明。

民主是一個詞，
民主可以被觀測並證明嗎？
筆者有實驗構想可以證明民主是對的：

1. 將一個容易淹水的地區分成 A、B 兩個區域。
2. 在 A、B 兩個區域裝設許多廣播器。
3. 準備警報按鈕，當按下按鈕時，廣播器會開始播放。
4. A 區域的廣播器會播放：「水災、水災，請儘速避難。」
B 區域的廣播器會播放：「國王好帥。」
5. 觀察居民是否避難。

這是一個簡單的實驗，這個實驗可以證明廣播器應該屬於人民而不應該屬於國王，筆者證明了民主真的是對的。

而在這個實驗中，筆者也證明了「文字」帶來的影響。

肆、龍的圖騰。

文字會對日常生活造成影響，
具體而言文字造成了什麼影響呢？
在這個小節，筆者將說明「龍的圖騰」。

在中華文化中，皇帝是真龍天子，皇帝的椅子上有龍的圖騰，皇帝的衣服上有龍的圖騰，龍的圖騰代表著皇帝的身分與正統性，而華人稱呼自己為龍的傳人，

「龍的傳人」就是為了民族、為了國家，我們要忠誠的意思，中華文化是忠孝節義，龍的圖騰團結著人民。

龍的圖騰代表著皇帝的正統性，
於是法律要生效時，必須要蓋上龍的印章，國家預算要發放時，必須要蓋上龍的印章，將軍的任命要蓋上龍的印章，錢幣上有龍的圖騰，寺廟中有龍的圖騰，節慶時會出現龍的圖騰，龍的圖騰影響著國家考試，教育的目的是讓下一代對國家有貢獻，龍的圖騰影響著個人興趣與科學發展，對國家沒有貢獻的理論科學難以發展。

當然，人民沒有言論自由，罵皇帝會連家人一起被殺，戲劇、歌曲、文學都不能觸怒皇帝，國家預算常常用來彰顯皇帝的偉大，向皇上跪拜才有飯吃。

龍的圖騰也在人們的心中，父母常常告訴子女要感謝國王，在人們的內心深處，代代相傳，「我們要感謝國王。」「先有國，才有

家，我們是龍的傳人。」

伍、廣播器的功用。

民主可以當飯吃嗎？

可以的，廣播器可以幫助人們吃飯，

當你發現黑心食品時，你按下了廣播器，廣播器保護了我們的食品安全，

當學校的營養午餐被貪心的校長換成劣等食材時，學生按下了廣播器，廣播器保護了學生的午餐。

廣播器有許多的功用，國家隊的教練性侵選手，軍中的不當管教，水利工程被偷工減料，商人把森林砍光了，工廠排放有毒物質到河裡，保險公司欺騙消費者，警察吃案，官員貪污亂花錢⋯⋯如果廣播器只是說著：「國王真偉大」，那麼弊案就會默默地發生。

以前人們沒有環保的觀念，

後來觀念與文字進入了廣播器，進入了人們心中，形成法律，形成消費習慣，形成了乾淨的故鄉，文字有強大的力量。

陸、新的圖騰。

生命的意義是忠誠，

龍的圖騰代表著威權的正統性。

而民主是對的嗎？

當我們要改變廣播器中的文字的時候，

新的文字是什麼呢？

「人生沒有答案」「民主是抽象的價值」，是嗎？

從「國王真偉大」改成「我不知道」，

從「國王一定是對的」改成「民主不一定是對的」，真是無奈，沒有人能找到一定是對的事，沒有人能證明民主一定是對的。

而筆者找到了，只要準備實驗組和對照組，

可以證明：「每個人都應該思考，每個人都應該關心故鄉。」

可以證明：「民主真的是對的。」

筆者的答案在一萬年以後依然會是對的，

這是應該代代相傳的文字，

這是應該進入廣播器的文字。

柒、結論。

民主是對的嗎？

民主只是一個詞嗎？

民主是抽象的價值嗎？

如果你們真的愛民主，

為什麼你們要把民主說成是主觀的價值？

學者們沒有盡到責任，

學校沒有指正「民主價值」。

文字是有力量的，

請大聲說出來吧！

「以前民主是價值，決長證明了民主是真的。」

Preface

The meaning of life is the most difficult question in human history.

Teachers say there is no standard answer to this question.

What a contradiction!

Going to school is meaningful,

But teachers are not sure if life has meaning;

The teacher stood on the podium,

Then he said, "What I said makes no sense."

The author discovered a simple but important thing,

"What are you going to do today?"

This means that people must fill today,

People must be responsible for "today",

The author discovered that life has meaning.

"People have to fill today."

But this answer is too abstract,

Specifically, what should we fill in?

So this article has many examples.

"People have to take responsibility for today."

So teachers should tell students:

"You should take responsibility for your life."

Schools should teach students the concept of goodness.

And the idea of goodness can have a huge impact.

Concrete examples, ideas of goodness, the impact of words.

The content of this book is these three topics:

"The meaning of life and the answers in the diary."

"Who are we? The meaning of life and identity."

"The meaning of life and the symbol of democracy."

The author wants to tell everyone:

In the past, people were not sure whether life had meaning;

Now, life really has meaning.

Jue Chang
2023、10、01

The Meaning of Life and the Answers in the Diary.

Section 1 : Introduction.

What do people life to do? What is the meaning of life? This is the most difficult question in human history. There have been philosophers who seriously challenged this question, but they went crazy after failing and committed suicide after failing.

When teenagers seriously think about the meaning of life, parents will feel worried and hope that their children will not think too much, just think superficially, and don't think deeply.

In daily life, the author discovered: "What do people life to do? This is an easy and relaxing question."

The author is not a newborn baby. "What should I do today? What should I do on the weekend? What should I do during consecutive holidays?" The author has answered this question many times.

The next "today" is not unknown,

The answers to "today" are already in the diary.

When I was hungry, I randomly found a restaurant to have lunch with my colleagues.

"What should I do today?"

This is an easy question, as easy as choosing lunch. This article will explain:

1. "Today" is a "blank" like hunger.

2. Answers in the diary.

3. Another way to prove.

4. Comparison and application.

In the diary, I have filled in "today",

This article will explain: "Concretely, what am I going to do today?"

This article will explain the paired hunger and beauty.

Section 2 : "Today" is a "blank" like hunger.

Why should humans think about the meaning of life?

In the past, humans misunderstood this topic,

The meaning of life is a noble topic,

So mediocre people do not need to think about this topic.

The meaning of life is the direction close to heaven,

Therefore, people who do not believe in God do not need to think about this topic.

"Meaning" is an idea imposed subjectively by humans. Human beings are restless in their hearts and lack direction. Human beings think wildly because they are uneasy, so they impose "meaning" on life, but what about "meaninglessness"? Why does life have to be "meaningful"? This is a human misunderstanding of this subject.

The author discovered: "Life is meaningful, and humans must fill today."

Today is a blank waiting to be filled,

And in the void lies hunger,

So everyone has to answer "today". Human beings will be hungry, and human beings must fill today. The following is the experimental method of "Humanity must fill today":

Experiment 1:

1. Prepare two identical rooms, Room A and Room B.

2. Prepare two volunteers, one to enter room A and the other to enter room B. Lock the doors.

3. Prepare the cameras to shoot the volunteers.

4. Send some food into room A every four hours, but there is no food in room B.

5. Record whether the volunteers have angry or painful reactions.

This is a simple experiment. This experiment can observe hunger. This is the characteristic of "today". What should we do today? There are things I have to do today, and I have to eat today.

Experiment 2:

1. Prepare two identical cages, cage A and cage B.

2. Prepare two dogs (or two human volunteers), one enters cage A and the other enters cage B, and lock the cages.

3. Prepare enough food and water for the two cages (A and B).

4. Prepare the cameras to shoot the dogs.

5. Take the dog in cage A out of the cage every day, walk for an hour, and then put it back in cage A. The dog in cage B cannot go out for

a walk.

6. Record the dogs' health status (appetite, activity, sleep, heartbeat, blood oxygen...).

This is a simple experiment. This experiment can prove: "Dogs (humans) have a need for exercise."

This is the characteristic of "today". What should we do today?

There are things I have to do today, and today I have to exercise.

Experiment 3:

1. Prepare two empty rooms, Room A and Room B.

2. Prepare two volunteers, one to enter room A and the other to enter room B, and lock the doors.

3. Put enough food and water in the two rooms, and then put a treadmill in each room.

4. Put a mobile phone with Internet access in room A. The volunteer in room A can call his friends, but room B does not have a mobile phone.

5. Let the volunteers live in the room for one month.

6. After one month, the volunteers will be given a health check (appetite, activity, sleep, heartbeat, blood oxygen, memory...).

This is a simple experiment. This experiment can prove: "Human beings need entertainment, and human beings have emotional needs."

This is the characteristic of "today". What should we do today?

Today I have things to do, today I have to find entertainment, today I have to find love and laughter.

Through these three experiments, it can be proved that "today" has characteristics. Today I have to eat, today I have to exercise, today I have to find entertainment.

"Today" is waiting for humans to fill in the colors. It is as irresistible as hunger. Humans must fill in the colors for "today". As long as humans still exist on the earth, humans must fill in the colors for "today".

Section 3 : Answers in the diary.

In the old concept, the future is unknown and life is unknown. Things you think are certain may change tomorrow.

And the author discovered: "Human beings must fill in the colors for today." This will still be true in the future.

The author wrote in his diary and in his book: "There is an answer to life. This is known. Human beings must fill in the colors for today."

Humanity must fill in the colors for today, so what specifically should be filled in?

The answer is: "Anything is OK.",

But "anything is fine" is not a specific answer.

So in this section, the author will use his own diary and things that have been done in human history as examples. These things are the answers to "what to fill in today?"

1. Human beings have the need to eat.

What am I going to eat today? The answer is "anything", specifically what did I eat? Opening the diary, I have eaten: fried rice, fried noodles, bread, burgers, sandwiches, steamed buns, mantou, dumplings, fried dough sticks, baked sweet potatoes, fried taro, puffs, pizza, mapo tofu, chocolate, ice cream, dorayaki, sushi, bubble tea, soy milk, jelly, pudding, salad, honey Cake, mirror cake, durian, seaweed rice rolls, zongzi, glutinous rice balls, curry, donuts, candied haws, potato chips, preserved eggs, congee, mayonnaise bamboo shoot, yokan, miso soup, instant noodles, pineapple cake, sachima, popcorn, hot pot, ramen, macaroni, cereal, shaved ice, tofu pudding, waffles, hot dogs, sausages, corn soup, sesame paste, herbal soup, truffle mushroom soup...

Opening the diary, what did I eat?

I like to eat soft cabbage. My mother often makes special cabbage dishes for me. It is very soft and thin. It is a special dish that cannot be eaten in any restaurant.

Once, my friend and I were on a remote mountain and randomly found a roadside cafe. Unexpectedly, we encountered super delicious coffee, which shocked both my friend and me.

Once, my club mates and I went camping and were cooking noodles on a cassette stove. Some of my mates complained that there wasn't enough noodles, so they added noodles to the pot. As a result, there were old noodles that were overcooked and new noodles that were undercooked. It was a meal full of laughter.

There is a coffee shop that I go to so often that I tried all the flavors on their menu.

I remember when I was a kid, I was eating instant noodles in the living room in the middle of the night. I lied to my grandpa and said I was too hungry and couldn't sleep. In fact, there was a TV program I wanted to watch...

The contents of the diary are all answers to the meaning of life.

In the diary, the author remembers that Buddha said: Heaven is important, eating is not. The author remembers that scholars were arguing about profit and justice. Those who pursue profit are villains, while those who pursue freedom and value are gentlemen.

The businessman said: Democracy cannot be eaten as food. The democratic martyrs said: Democracy is like air. Although it cannot be eaten, it is very important.

And the author discovered: "Eating is really important."

Because eating is really important, I have to thank the farmer, the chef, the driver, the cashier at the bakery...

Because eating is really important, we must care about taxes and the country, and the people must ask the country to take care of the people.

There are answers to the meaning of life in the diary. Eating is really important. We must care about the country and we must eat together.

In history, in order to eat, humans developed trade and learned to cooperate. In order to eat, humans invented cans, refrigerators, and microwaves. Farmers worked hard to grow more delicious fruits, and chefs thought of new menus. The author lives in a convenient civilization.

How can we answer the question of eating? Rich menus, advanced technology, a society that cares about each other, and convenient civilization, civilization is right in front of me. Specifically, what should we fill in today? There are answers in history, and the civilization in front of us is the specific answer.

2. Human beings have a need for exercise.

What should I do today? The answer is "anything". Specifically, what kind of exercise did I do?

Opening the diary, I have done: running, basketball, baseball, football, volleyball, table tennis, tennis, badminton, high jump,

skipping rope, long jump, shot put, yo-yo, tug-of-war, Tai Chi, fighting with classmates with brooms, cheerleading, Climbing trees, swinging, gymnastics, swimming, hide-and-seek, dancing, riding bicycles, skating, push-ups, dodgeball, playing slides, playing seesaw, massage, rowing...

Opening the diary, The exercises I do most frequently are walking and running.

So boring! The author once felt this way when I was in junior high school. At that time, it was still a cramming education. The school did not encourage thinking and encouraged memorization. Because it was too boring, I went to the sports field. It was really suitable. When I was bored, I did what my classmates thought was boring. I can run 10,000 meters for fifty minutes.

I adjust my breathing, repeat movements, and forget about exams. I find happiness. This is a great discovery. "How to get rid of the boredom in my heart? How to feel happy?" This is a question that many scholars are challenging, and the author's diary has the answer.

Opening the diary, the author remembers the doubts he had when he was in junior high school, between a child and an adult, wondering about the future.

The author remembers that some classmates had similar problems. They were also confused about the future. They had plenty of energy but didn't know where to spend it. Let's brawl! Let's drag! Seek excitement! The teacher is powerless, no one can answer life, no one can answer the future.

This difficult question has a simple answer. The future is certain. The author discovered: "Human beings need exercise." This will still be true in the future. This is the answer to life.

You can try running, you can try playing basketball, you can try to catch the monsters in the AR game on the street, the answer is "anything ", go and give it a try!

The newspapers in the library record the glorious moments. The author's hometown loves baseball. When the international competition happens, we have a common feeling. What is the answer to life? The news introduces great players who dedicated their lives to baseball. What's the answer for the future? In the future, if my hometown does not perish, people in my hometown will continue to play baseball. Humans are no longer primitive. Humans invented baseball. Specifically, what should we fill in today? Baseball is concrete, baseball is the concrete answer.

3. Human beings have entertainment needs.

What should I do today? The answer is "anything". My heart will be hungry. Specifically, what do I fill in my heart?

Opening the diary, I have done: reading, writing, photography, graffiti, reading comics, watching animation, playing video games, playing Go, reading newspapers, watching TV, listening to music, admiring flowers, admiring the moon, watching fireworks, kneading clay, Origami airplanes, guessing puzzles, performing magic tricks, playing pranks, watching cross talk, reading memes, playing dominoes, hide and seek, playing cards, blowing bubbles, talking to electric fans, small science experiments, collecting stamps, petting cats, shopping, visit friends, go online , hold a robot in my left hand and a dinosaur in my right hand, let the robot fight with the dinosaur...

Opening the history of the mobile phone, in the communication software, the author's mother often says good morning to me, and I often send her some interesting news. For example, the puppy got lost and went to the police station to ask for help.

For example, The bear in the zoo walks around on two legs, and it's suspected that it's a part-time worker in disguise.

For example, some idiots called the Meteorological Bureau to complain about the bad weather... The author's mother has retired. I taught her how to use a mobile phone, how to play music, and how to search for videos. Some books can be read on the mobile phone without going to the library.

What should I fill my heart with? This is the answer, good morning in communication software is the answer.

What should I do today? The answer is in the library. When you walk into the library, there are little flowers taken care of by the staff at the counter. Beauty is today's answer. There are today's new newspapers in the newspaper area. Retired old uncles are queuing up to read the news. This is today's answer. The library has a new book section, and librarians recommend some new books to readers. The library also has old classics. The story of the Golden Ax and the Silver Ax and the story of the Three Little Pigs will always be passed down. There are students in the library writing reports. If the topic was free play, what would the students write?

Specifically, what do I fill in today?

Last summer, I went swimming, had ice cream, and went to the night market with my friends. Are you going to do the same things this summer? Will students do the same things ten years from now?

People's hearts will be hungry. What did the ancients fill in their hearts? The ancients left behind classics, Beethoven, Mozart, Shakespeare... This is the specific answer. The answer is music and literature. Literature is the answer to the meaning of life.

Section 4 : Another way to prove.

Does life have meaning? This is the most difficult question in human history. In the past, no one could prove that there was or was not, but the author proved that life is meaningful. The author has prepared experimental methods that can prove that nature has laws and that humans have things they must do in life. Human beings must eat, exercise, find entertainment, and satisfy their emotions.

The author's experimental method can be observed with a camera, but some readers will still feel doubtful. The author has given specific examples, but some readers will still feel doubtful.

People are always afraid of life,The answer is already in front of us, but there are still readers who are doubting: Is life really meaningful? Has Jue Chang answered this question?

Is there a better way to persuade someone than facts? The author has presented the facts, but people still feel doubtful in their hearts. Therefore, in this section, the author will propose another method to prove that life is meaningful. The method is as follows:

As long as I can deny the two sentences: "Life is meaningless" and

"It is uncertain whether life has meaning",

I can prove that life is meaningful.

Section 5 : Comparison and application.

The topic "The meaning of life" is related to daily life and has many applications in daily life. However, the sentence "life is meaningless" cannot have any application. The author discovered that life is meaningful. What changes will the author's discovery bring? This section is comparison and application.

1. Why should people think?

In authoritarian times, kings taught people to obey, but now schools encourage students to think, why is it wrong to obey and right to think? Teachers in school always say: "There is no standard answer to life. Teachers are not saints. Teachers do not have the answer to life. You should think. You should find your own answer."

And this is wrong. "Teachers do not have the answer" This sentence is meaningless. The sentence "Teachers have no answer" only infers that thinking is not necessarily correct.

"Teachers are stupid" and "Students should think"

These two things are completely unrelated.

Only "life is meaningful and you should enrich your mind" can we deduce the conclusion that "people should think".

2. Why do universities need general education?

Why do universities need general courses? Are general courses meaningful? When general education teachers mention the meaning of life, they always say: "The meaning of life is a difficult question. Some people think life is meaningful, and some people think life is meaningless. The purpose of general education courses is to lead students listen to both sides." How strange! You're not sure if life has meaning, but general education classes do? The sentence "It is uncertain whether life has meaning" is meaningless. "It is uncertain whether life has meaning" can only infer: "It is meaningless to respect others and it is meaningless to understand others."

It should be: "Life is meaningful, people should enrich their minds , and people should enrich their perspectives of appreciating beauty."

Life is certain to have meaning, and then general education courses are certain to have meaning.

General education teachers, please don't stand on the podium and say that you are not sure whether general education courses are meaningful.

3. Literature is meaningful.

The author discovered that literature is meaningful. This is a simple discovery, but have writers discovered this? It is very contradictory. Some writers say that life is meaningful. And some writers lamented life, sighing: they have worked hard all their lives but left nothing.

How strange! Literary writers write articles, and then say in the article that life is meaningless, "this article is meaningless." If literature is meaningless, then why should students study literature?

4. Reasons for patriotism.

In a dictatorship, the king will ask the people to be loyal, but in a democracy, you can be patriotic or not. There is no standard answer in life. If a person says he has a standard answer, he says he represents morality,

If he imposes a moral standard on others, then this person is a threat.

"Only dictators and religious charlatans claim that there's a definitive answer to morality."

This is an old concept, which is contradictory. People in democratic countries do not need to be patriotic, which is really strange. The author discovered that people have a need to eat. We must eat together, we must thank farmers, we must care about taxes, and we must care about the country. The author has found a common answer.

5. A Common Core Idea.

In a democracy, everyone can make their own claims, right? So, can a presidential candidate regard dictatorship as a political opinion? What if a dictatorial candidate is elected? This is ridiculous. Of course, if someone who advocates dictatorship is elected, the country will move towards dictatorship and democracy will be eliminated.

Democracy cannot deny itself. If we don't have a common core idea, and half the people support democracy and half the people support dictatorship, our country will be in chaos.

For the same reason, democracy cannot deny itself, and life cannot deny itself.

You should not think that life is meaningless.

6. The rise of artificial intelligence.

There are often plots like this in science fiction novels: "With the rise of artificial intelligence, humans no longer have to work. It seems happy, but humans begin to degenerate and corrupt, and then the progressive civilization destroys itself."This topic in science fiction novels may soon be come true, in the face of the rise of artificial intelligence, teachers should tell students: "Life is meaningful, people must exercise themselves, and people must enrich their minds ." "Life is meaningful, we must eat together, and we must ask the country to take care of those who fall. People have to keep caring."

7. Parents' wishes.

When welcoming a new life, parents will imagine their children's future and make wishes. One common wish is: "I will not ask my children to have any great achievements, as long as you can grow up safely and cherish yourself, You can do whatever you want."

There is no basis for wishes, and the author has proved this. The answer is "anything is OK", but you must exercise and you must cherish yourself.

Section 6 : Conclusion.

What should we going to do today? What should people life to do ? The author found the answer. I discovered that today is a "blank" like hunger. This can be captured with a camera. Human beings have needs. Human beings need to eat, exercise, find entertainment and satisfy their emotions. Human beings must fill in the colors of today, and what exactly should be filled in? The author uses the answers in the diary as examples. The author has proved that life is meaningful.

"Life is meaningless" and

"It is uncertain whether life has meaning",

These two sentences will have no application.

"If the meaning of life has no connection with general education, then general education teachers, please refrain from discussing the meaning of life. If the meaning of life is indeed related to general education, it implies that life has meaning."

Please don't stand on the podium and say I don't know,

Please don't say: I'm not sure whether life has meaning, and I'm not sure whether general education classes have meaning. Please stop your stupid self-denial.

In the past, no one could prove that life is really meaningful. Now that life is really meaningful, who has answered this question? Please say it out loudly: "Life really has meaning, Jue Chang has solved the question."

Who are we? The meaning of life and identity.

Section 1 : Preface.

The author's hometown is Taiwan. Taiwan used to be authoritarian, and Taiwan is now moving toward democracy.

A Taiwanese politician said: "Democracy is our DNA."

This is wrong. Democracy is not something you are born with.

In the past, Taiwanese people loved dictators deeply, treating them as parents and saviors.

The dictator was once a hero in the words of teachers, and parents told their children to be as great as that hero when they grow up.

Who are we? We are the children and disciples of dictators.

Philosophers say: There is no common answer to the meaning of life, everyone's answer is different.

This is wrong. There is a common answer to the meaning of life. The meaning of life is loyalty to the emperor and patriotism.

Sacrificing oneself to achieve the success of the country, there are many people who are willing to sacrifice their lives for the king.

Listening to God's words is also the common answer to the meaning of life. In the name of God, believers form a big family. Believers are willing to sacrifice their lives for God. Both dictators and gods once formed big families.

In the big family of dictators, some people shout for freedom, but does freedom mean non-interference?

Can we form a new family?

"Who are we?" Is there an answer to this question?

This article will explain:

1. The common points of life.

2. What should we fill in?

3. What is goodness?

4. Comparison and application.

"Who are we?" is how to build a complete personality for the next generation. This article will explain the "reasons for kindness" and "the reasons for unity."

Section 2 : The common points of life.

"Who are we?" Philosophers say this is a difficult question,

"What kind of people should we be?"

Teachers say: Everyone is different and there is no standard answer in life.

This is a contradiction, there is no standard answer in life, but we should unite to fight against dictatorship.

In order to solve this contradiction, the author discovered that human beings have something in common. The following is the author's experimental method:

1. Just prepare the experimental group and the control group. The control group is a room without food. The experimental group will send some food into the room every four hours, and then observe the volunteers in the room. This experiment can prove that human beings have something in common. Everyone gets hungry.

2. Prepare the experimental group and the control group. The control group is an empty room. The experimental group's room has a TV, comics and mobile phones. Then observe the volunteers in the room. This experiment can prove that human beings have something in common, and the human heart will be hungry, humans have emotional needs.

3. Prepare the experimental group and control group,

The control group is humans living on Earth.

The experimental group is humans drifting in space,

This experiment can prove that

Human beings need land, human beings have something in common,

We are earthlings.

Who are we? The answer is right in front of you,

We can observe humans,

Human characteristics can be discovered after observation,

Humans will be hungry,

Human beings need love and laughter,

Human beings need land and hometown,

Who are we? We are earthlings.

Section 3 : Another answer.

Who are we?

We were all babies once,

Only crying for milk,

In need of parental care,

Needs lullabies and stories from parents.

We were once like a blank sheet of paper,

Can't speak, can't write my own name,

There is no answer to "Who am I?" on the white paper.

After receiving education from parents and teachers,

After growth and exploration, the blank paper is no longer blank.

"Who am I?" "Who are we?"

There is another answer.

What should be filled in the blanks?

My mother sang folk songs for me. There are several folk songs that have been sung for a long time in my hometown. My mother cooked for me. There were several common dishes. Everyone in my hometown has eaten the same dishes.

The story of the three little pigs,

The story of the tortoise and the hare,

My mother told me many stories.

What should be filled in the blanks?

After learning to speak,

Children also learn to quarrel and get angry,

Therefore, mothers must teach their children the concepts of good and evil.

Fill in the blanks with education,

Fill in the blanks with the answers to "What is good?" and "What kind of people should we be?"

Section 4 : What is goodness?

What is goodness? What's great?

What kind of people should we become?

Mothers buy biographies of world greats for their children,

Beethoven, Lincoln, Wright brothers, Edison, Gandhi, Nightingale...

Mothers say these are great people, and mothers want their children to be little Edisons.

What is goodness?

Religion is good;

Jesus, Buddha, Allah and many gods are good,

In the name of God, believers pray together, pray before eating, pray before going to bed, pray for each other, believers celebrate the birthday of the saint together, and believers sing hymns together.

When you are dumped, other believers send you warmth. When you need to apply for college, other believers will discuss it with you. When you feel troubled and regretful, there will be older believers who listen quietly.

When hospitalized, other believers come to visit, religion unites people, God is good, and people are children of God.

What is goodness?

Patriotism is good, selfishness is evil,

Loyalty is good, questioning is evil.

Disloyal generals will bring war,

Only faithfulness is the answer to peace.

Don't be selfish, everything belongs to the king,

The king said: "My people! My country! You belong to me and I love you."

Mom's storybook contains stories about knights,

The brave knight protects the king and the people,

We remember our ancestors,

Grandfather's grandfather died for the country,

Because of their sacrifices, we have our current home.

Selfishness is cowardly and shameful,

A person's life is small and meaningless,

Life is meaningful only if you live for the country.

Give up the self and become a group,

We are one, we are the sword of the King.

What is goodness?

The king is good and religion is good? Really?

Can't people be selfish?

Think about it more deeply,

Is there a standard answer to kindness?

Good and evil often change depending on the position,

often change with time,

The future is unknown,

Humanity has not found "True Justice."

Is white supremacy right?

Is equality between black and white right?

Dr. King said: "I have a dream."

But dreams cannot be proven,

Dr. King did not say that he was necessarily right.

Does life have meaning? Life is meaningless?

When students commit suicide because they can't find the meaning of life,

The principal said: "Teachers are not saints. Teachers do not have the answers to life."

You should care about your hometown,

But can't people be selfish?

Democracy is precious,

But is the majority right?

You should think,

But can't people be mediocre?

Universal value is a lie;

Parents should not decide their children's lives,

You are you, I am me,

There is no standard answer to kindness;

"Who are we?" There is no answer.

Section 5 : The author's answer.

Humanity has not found true justice,

The future is unknown,

Human beings have not found something that is definitely right.

And the author discovered: "The future is known."

Just prepare the experimental group and the control group,

The control group maintains the environment, and the experimental group does not maintain the environment.

This proves that humans should protect the earth,

This will still be true in ten thousand years.

Just prepare the experimental group and the control group,

It can be proved that people will be hungry,

People should eat together and protect their hometown together.

Just prepare the experimental group and the control group,

It can prove that people's hearts will be hungry,

People have to think, people have to fill it with love and laughter.

The author has found true justice,

People have to think, people have to care about their hometown, and people have to protect the earth. This will still be right ten thousand years from now.

"Who are we?"

Children are like blank sheets of paper waiting for their parents' education.

Parents should tell their children what they should and shouldn't do.

Parents should teach their children the concept of kindness,

But have humans found something that is definitely right?

Do humans ever find something that is definitely right and then tell their children?

Yes, I found it,

Just prepare experimental and control groups to demonstrate:

People have to think, people have to care about their hometown, and people have to protect the earth.

When it comes to filling in a sound personality and good concepts,

We should tell the next generation:

"Science has proven that people should think and care about their hometown."

From generation to generation, what we pass on is science,

We are people of science.

Section 6 : Comparison and application.

Who are we? The author discovered that human beings have something in common.

We are earthlings.

What kind of people should we become? How should we educate the next generation?

The author discovered something that will still be true in the future.

We should tell the next generation: "As long as we prepare

experimental groups and control groups, we can prove that people should think and care about their hometown."

We are people of science.

The author's discovery is a simple but important discovery.

This section is comparison and application：

1. The debate between loyalty and democracy.

In the process of moving from authoritarianism to democracy, there are often scenes like this. Grandpa said: The king has great favors for the people,

And teenagers shout for democracy and freedom. Is democracy just a political system? Loyalty is belief, and promoting democracy means changing old beliefs.

But paradoxically,

Democracy means freedom of belief. Grandpa believes in loyalty. Young people believe in freedom. Freedom should tolerate loyalty. The democratic martyrs did not say that democracy must be right. The democratic martyrs said: There is no standard answer in life, we want freedom.

2. God said.

Because of the will of God and the King, you must obey the law. Because the king is the chosen one, you must be loyal.

When people want to pursue freedom, the democratic martyrs also said similar words:

Because "God says human rights are right, God says freedom is right, God says democracy is right."

So we should be democratic.

What a contradiction,

God is the only righteousness,

People have freedom of belief.

What a contradiction,

Freedom is human instinct. Human beings loved freedom two thousand years ago.

The Bible says about democracy, right?

3. Confucius.

In Chinese culture, Confucius is the greatest teacher, the teacher of all teachers. People once fought with each other like wild beasts. In the chaos, Confucius said: "The king should behave like a king, and the ministers should behave like ministers.

Fathers should behave like fathers, and children should behave like children. "

Confucius advocated "loyalty" and we should listen to the words of the king and parents.

Confucius brought order,

Most Chinese are disciples of Confucius.

In the future, should we educate the next generation about "loyalty" or "democracy"? And there is no "democracy" in Confucius's books. Are we still Confucius's disciples?

4. Love Taiwan.

The author's hometown is Taiwan. There was a debate in Taiwan: "Can Taiwanese not love Taiwan?"

Democracy is freedom. You can care about your hometown, or you can be selfish and not love Taiwan. There is no standard answer in life, but if someone does not love Taiwan, he will be scolded:

"How dare you not love Taiwan."

There is a contradiction. "There is no standard answer to life" is in conflict with "Taiwanese people have a common life".

And the author found a common answer, and the author found a reason for unity.

5. Check the facts.

Dr. King said: "I have a dream",

When people discuss public affairs, in the old concept,

No one is "neutral, rational, and objective." Don't lie. You are subjective, and so am I. Everyone has his own position, so Dr. King shared his dream. If many people agree with his dream, his dreams can form policies.

In the new concept, when people's opinions differ, we have to check whether the opinions are consistent with the facts. "Facts" are the basis for integrating everyone's opinions.

6. Reasons for goodness.

What kind of people should we become?

Parents tell their children "the reasons for being good",

Because Santa Claus will deliver gifts, you have to be a good child.

Because there will be bogeymen in the middle of the night, and bogeymen will eat misbehaving children, so you have to be a good child.

Jesus and Buddha talked about heaven and hell, so you have to be a good boy, Who are we? We are the good little kids that Santa loves, and the reasons for being good are fairy tales.

And who has found true justice?

Who has found a reason to be good?

The author found it,

The author proved: "People should care about their hometown."

7. News of suicide.

Taiwan University sometimes encounters such tragedies:

Because they could not find the meaning of life, some students committed suicide.

And how do teachers teach the meaning of life?

"The meaning of life is an unsolvable question,

No one can prove whether life has meaning."

Or

"Life really has meaning,

Jue Chang solved this question."

It's really cruel. Many teachers are unwilling to tell students that "life is really meaningful."

Many teachers are disciples of Jesus, Buddha, and Confucius.

So they are reluctant to speak out about this new concept.

Section 7 : Conclusion.

Who are we?

In the past, people knelt and worshiped,

People are children of the King and God,

In the future, will people continue to kneel and worship?

You have your beliefs, I have mine,

Belief is free, right?

So how do schools educate the next generation?

Goodness is loyalty, goodness is listening to the king, or goodness is returning to heaven. How should we teach ?

Who are we?

People should think and care about their hometown, right?

Yes, we are earthlings and we should care about the earth.

People should think and care about their hometown, right?

Yes, just prepare the experimental group and the control group,

This can be proven to be true, we follow "Truth",

We are people of science.

The meaning of life and the symbol of democracy.

Section 1 : Preface.

The author's hometown is currently holding an election (2023, Taiwan), "Defend universal values and defend democratic values." The candidates shouted loudly, and the candidates believed:

If I shout louder, I stand for justice.

And what exactly are universal values? Why are you fighting over subjective values? In the past, martyrs have sacrificed their lives for "democratic values". It is really a contradiction. Democracy is very precious, but democracy is an illusory value. When public figures said on stage that democracy was a subjective value, scholars did not correct them. Scholars did not know whether democracy was subjective or objective.

Democracy is just an abstract word;

Just an enshrined symbol ,

Yeah?

So what is the difference between worshiping democracy and worshiping dictatorship?

Can democracy keep people fed?

This article will explain: "Democracy can keep people fed."

The author prepared a democratic control group and an authoritarian experimental group so that democracy could be proven.

This article will explain:

1. In the past, democracy was a value.

2. Objective proof.

3. Symbol of authority.

4. New symbol.

This article will explain that symbols are the answer to "How should we live?"

This article will explain the influence of symbols.

Section 2 : Is democracy a value?

Is democracy a subjective value?

Is democracy definitely right?

People say that democracy is a universal value. It is really strange. There is no right or wrong in subjective values. It is really strange. The universal value is loyalty, right?

In this section, the author will explain:

"Why did people think democracy was a value in the past?"

Based on the will of the King and God, the people should obey the law.

In the past, the king was good, and the king was also the distributor of wealth. The people had to kneel down to the king to have food to eat. When they knelt down to eat, the people were bullied, so some people stood up to resist, and they shouted for freedom.

They don't care about food and life safety. Freedom is value, profit and justice are in conflict. Those who pursue interests are villains, and those who pursue value are gentlemen.

So a contradiction arises,

Some people say: "Democracy cannot be eaten as food."

Some people say: "Democracy is a noble value."

"Democracy is a noble value and cannot be eaten as food."

People think democracy is a value.

Why is democracy a value?

Because loyalty is wrong,

There is no standard answer in life,

Everyone can express their opinion,

Democracy is about subjective opinions and values.

You can support dictatorship, you can also support democracy,

Democracy is just a choice.

The future is unknown and no one is necessarily right.

Is majority rule better than listening to the king?

uncertain,

But when faced with an unknown future,

The martyrs believed in democracy,

Democracy is subjective belief, choice, opinion, and value.

Section 3 : Objective proof.

Democracy is a word,

Can democracy be observed and proven?

The author has experimental ideas that can prove that democracy is right:

1. Find an area that is often flooded and divide the area into two areas, A and B.

2. Install many broadcasters in areas A and B.

3. Prepare the alarm button, when the button is pressed, the broadcasters will start playing.

4.The broadcasters in area A will play: "Flood, flood, please evacuate as soon as possible."

The broadcasters in area B will play: "The king is so handsome."

5. Observe whether residents are taking refuge.

This is a simple experiment. This experiment can prove that the broadcasters should belong to the people and not to the king. The author proves that democracy is really right.

In this experiment, the author also proved the impact of "words".

Section 4 : The Loong's Symbol.

Words have an impact on daily life,

Specifically, what impact did words have?

In this section, the author will explain "The Symbol of the Loong". (Loong is Chinese Dragon.)

In Chinese culture, the emperor is the incarnation of the Loong , the emperor is the true son of heaven, the throne of the emperor bears the symbol of the Loong, and the clothes of the emperor display the symbol of the Loong. The symbol of the Loong represents the emperor's identity and legitimacy. Chinese people refer to themselves as descendants of the Loong.

"Descendants of the Loong" means "For the nation and the country, we must be loyal."Chinese culture values loyalty, and the symbol of the Loong unites the people.

The symbol of the Loong represents the legitimacy of the emperor,

So when the law is to take effect, it must be stamped with the Loong's seal. When the national budget is to be released, it must be stamped with the Loong's seal. The appointment of generals must be stamped with the Loong's seal.

Currency features the symbol of the Loong, and temples bear the symbol of the Loong. The symbol of the Loong appears during festivals. The symbol of the Loong influences national examinations. The purpose of education is to ensure the next generation contribute to the nation. The symbol of the Loong influences personal interests and scientific development. Personal interests that do not contribute to the country are not loved by parents, and theoretical science that does not contribute to the country are not loved by the emperor.

Of course, people do not have freedom of speech. If you criticize the emperor, your family will be killed. Drama, song, and literature cannot offend the emperor. The national budget is often used to highlight the emperor's greatness. Only by kneeling down to the emperor can you eat.

The symbol of the Loong is also in people's hearts. Parents often tell their children to thank the king. Deep in people's hearts, it is passed down from generation to generation, "We should thank the king." "First there is a country, then there is a family. We are the Descendants of the Loong."

Section 5 : Function of broadcaster.

Can't democracy be eaten as food?

Yes, the broadcaster can help people eat,

When you discovered illegal food, you pressed the broadcaster. The broadcaster protected our food safety.

When the school's nutritious lunch was replaced by inferior ingredients by the greedy principal, the students pressed the broadcaster, and the broadcaster protected the students' lunch.

Broadcasters have many functions, national team coaches sexually assault players, improper discipline in the military, water conservancy projects are cut corners, businessmen cut down forests, factories discharge toxic substances into rivers, insurance companies deceive consumers, and police collude with gangs, officials are corrupt and waste the budget... If the broadcaster just says: "The King is so great," then the tragedies will happen silently.

In the past, people did not have the concept of environmental protection.

Later, concepts and words entered the broadcaster and entered people's hearts, forming laws, forming consumption habits, and forming a clean hometown. Words have powerful power.

Section 6 : New Symbol.

The meaning of life is loyalty,

The Loong's Symbol represents authoritarian legitimacy.

And is democracy right?

When we want to change the words in the broadcaster,

What are the new words?

"There is no answer in life" "Democracy is an abstract value", right?

From "The King is so great" to "I don't know",

Change from "The king must be right" to "Democracy is not necessarily right."

People have experienced despair,

No one can find something that is definitely right, and no one can prove that democracy is definitely right.

And the author found it, just prepare the experimental group and the control group,

It can be proved: "Everyone should think and everyone should care about their hometown."

It can prove: "Democracy is really right."

The author's answer will still be correct ten thousand years from now.

These are words that should be passed down from generation to generation,

These are the words that should go into the broadcaster.

Section 7 : Conclusion.

Is democracy right?

Is democracy just a word?

Is democracy an abstract value?

If you really love democracy, why do you describe democracy as a subjective value?

Scholars have failed in their responsibilities;

The school did not correct "democratic value".

Words are powerful;

Please speak up!

"Democracy was a value in the past, and Jue Chang proved that democracy is true."

生命的意義與日記中的答案
The Meaning of Life and the Answers in the Diary
（中英雙語版）

作　　者／決長（Jue Chang）
出版者／美商 EHGBooks 微出版公司
發行者／美商漢世紀數位文化公司
臺灣學人出版網：http：／／www.TaiwanFellowship.org
地　　址／106 臺北市大安區敦化南路 2 段 1 號 4 樓
電　　話／02-2701-6088 轉 616-617
印　　刷／漢世紀古騰堡®數位出版 POD 雲端科技
出版日期／2024 年 2 月
總經銷／Amazon.com
臺灣銷售網／三民網路書店：http：／／www.sanmin.com.tw
　　　　　三民書局復北店
　　　　　　　地址／104 臺北市復興北路 386 號
　　　　　　　電話／02-2500-6600
　　　　　三民書局重南店
　　　　　　　地址／100 臺北市重慶南路一段 61 號
　　　　　　　電話／02-2361-7511
全省金石網路書店：http：／／www.kingstone.com.tw
定　　價／新臺幣 450 元（美金 15 元／人民幣 100 元）

2024 年版權美國登記，未經授權不許翻印全文或部分及翻譯為其他語言或文字。
2024 © United States, Permission required for reproduction, or translation in whole or part.

www.ingramcontent.com/pod-product-compliance
Lightning Source LLC
LaVergne TN
LVHW041713060526
838201LV00043B/716